Praise for Poetry As Therapy

'I wish I had this book 20 years ago! The simplicity but power this book has is mind blowing. The words of the poems resonated so deeply and then the deeper life lesson relating to the poem has given me so many breakthroughs from the space to explore my own thoughts. This book is a blessing to the world!'

Natalie Smith – Spiritual Coach

'These poems and invitations to reflect, offer a chance to connect to a more creative, deeper and more kind place within ourselves. Sarah shares insights gained through personal experience and a commitment to living a rich and fulfilling life that accepts challenge as part of being human. Wonderful.'

Andy Gillies, Spiritual - Staff Care and Person Centred Care Lead - NHS Ayrshire & Arran

'Heartfelt and filled with widsom. Sarah shares an artful way of self-enquiry to help us connect more deeply with ourselves and our emotions.'

Samantha Heaney - Embodiment Coach, Facilitator and Energy Work

'I found this book an amazing comfort. Each poem and technique is incredible for self-growth. Anyone looking to heal areas of your life then this book is for you!'

Sharon Florea, Healer, Medium and Bereavement Counsellor

'What a fascinating read that took me on an unexpected self-reflection journey. With each poem that I read I went deeper within. Truly inspired and ready to act.'

Gerry McGread, Founder – Everything Connected

Poetry As Therapy

A collection of short poems based on observations of life and the life lessons I have learned along the way

Author: Sarah Barbour

For information www.sarahbarbourcoaching.com

Editor: Penny Thresher /Corner House Words
Project Manager: Leanne MacDonald / She Speaks Media

Sarah Barbour Publishing - 2022
ISBN: 9798440300132

This book is dedicated to the memory of
John Anthony Heaney
Thank you for the life lessons and inspiration for many of these poems.

Contents

Introduction

Introduction

I want to start by thanking you for buying this book. My intention for the book is to share my thoughts and observations of life through writing short poems and sharing the lessons I have learned. I don't have all the answers, but I have learned that nobody does. We are all figuring things out as we go through life.

Writing poems is a form of therapy for me. Every poem I have written has started with a question or an observation. When writing a poem I ask a question, connect with my own intuition or experience and try to find the answer. Most of the answers are already within us; we just need to learn to trust ourselves and to quieten the noise, so we can connect to and hear our inner wisdom.

We can learn so much about ourselves by asking questions and being open to the answers that appear. This may require a little work on our part; a bit of self-exploration and a willingness to do the work required to move forward. In my experience, this is what will set you free and give you confidence to live the life you want to live; free from the fear and limiting beliefs that may have held you back.

I was in my 40s before I was ready to do self-exploration. Growing up a shy child, I tended to follow other's leads and enjoyed friendships with people who were more outgoing than I was. I was a good listener and enjoyed helping my friends with relationship dramas. I became a good fixer, always looking outwards and helping others.

When I did look inwards, it was to fix what I perceived were my shortcomings rather than exploring why I felt a certain way. I was hyper-aware of what I felt I was not good at. Lacking in confidence, I got nervous in certain social situations, and I could be self-critical. So how did I combat that? By trying to be perfect! I tried to project to the world that I had my shit together. That I could be really good at my job, be the perfect girlfriend, wife, mother. The list goes on and on. But looking back, all I did was put myself under a great deal of pressure. I believed that external factors were causing my stress. I had no insight into the fact I was the one putting myself under pressure.

Always happy to offer help to others, I was not good at asking others for help. I would sit on my feelings and keep trying harder. Only if something were really bothering me, would I get my journal out, write about how I was feeling and brainstorm by asking questions to try and find the answers. It worked well and helped me process feelings but was always a last-resort option when it should have been a regular and effective habit. I believed, incorrectly, that I should be able to fix all my problems in my head.

In 2021, when I started writing poems during lockdown, I noticed that I often asked questions and tried to figure out answers in my poems. I began to realise that writing poems had become a way of connecting to and processing my feelings. And this time I was slowing down, trusting myself and connecting to my intuition without judgement.

The idea of writing a book started to formulate in my mind when the country went into lockdown in response to the Coronavirus Pandemic. Prior to the pandemic, I had worked in a corporate role within the NHS for 25 years and my life was comfortable and structured. I had a good job, earned good money, was married to my best friend and had a supportive family and friends.

Like many other people, I felt a huge amount of fear when we were forced into lockdown due to the pandemic. Through my role in the NHS, I was hearing first-hand about all the preparations and contingency plans that were required to be put into place and I felt quite overwhelmed. All I wanted to do was hide from it all and keep safe with my family.

Work life was manic but I was able to work from the safety of my home. Due to the restrictions, I had time to slow down when I was not working. This was unusual for me as I was always doing something and very rarely just sat still.

This gave me time to stop and contemplate. I realised how fast paced my life was and how I rarely ever stopped to think about what I was doing or how I really felt. Fear had been a big part in my life and I had been trying to control fear by being safe. By making safe choices, by not taking any risks, by staying in my comfort zone. This was particularly true when it came to my career. When I really explored that feeling I realised that I felt safe but uninspired. As a child I had been a dreamer always wondering what was around the corner, but I had disconnected from my creativity and my daydreams.

It was during this time that I started writing poems. I wrote a poem about fear and found the process really enjoyable, cathartic, and therapeutic. I shared the poems I wrote with my husband and my sister who both encouraged me to keep writing and to share my poems with others.

I wrote poems regularly and shared them on my Instagram page and I liked it when people were able to relate to what I had described within my poems. I always loved helping people to see their potential and to overcome obstacles. It lit me up to think that it would be possible to do this for a stranger through the simple act of writing a poem.

Around this time, I worked with Natalie Smith, a brilliant Embodiment Coach and during one of our sessions, we discussed the idea of putting my poems into a book. I also signed up to complete an Advanced Certificate in Coaching Practice through Mindful Talent as I recognised I could undertake self-development, whilst training to do something that I would really enjoy.

The more I learned about myself through coaching, the more poems I was able to produce as I reflected on various emotions and feelings. I felt so passionate about coaching and writing!   I realised that I was doing something that I really enjoyed and how great that felt. I began to understand why I never wanted to progress at work. I had been given so many opportunities that I did not take. I knew what I didn't want but it was not until I started to explore coaching and writing that I discovered what I did want; what I was good at; and what lit me up on the inside.

In September 2021, I lost my dad in a tragic motorbike accident. He was 63 years old when he died. The shock we felt as a family was overwhelming, and it was difficult to process our feelings. During this time, I wrote poems to express my pain, shock, and loss. It helped me to have an outlet for the huge emotions I was feeling. I did not know how to cope with the grief and shock but writing poems really helped me to process my feelings. I had so many questions and had to learn to trust my intuition to know how to move forward.

I shared the poems with my family who could relate to what I was expressing as they were experiencing the same feelings. My mum spent time speaking to others experiencing grief on-line and she shared some of my poems to help other people relate and process how they were feeling.

I try to offer some hope in my poems; a reminder that life is a combination of good and bad; that each of us are stronger than we believe and if we keep moving forward, we will find a way through.

I decided to incorporate self-enquiry questions into this book for each poem to allow you, the reader, the opportunity to go a little deeper with themes covered in the poems that you can relate to.

I truly believe that it is through self-enquiry that we really learn to know ourselves better. We are never too old to learn more about ourselves, to start a new chapter or to live our dream life. We have everything we need within ourselves to achieve anything we set our minds too.

Life Lockdown

Life so busy, schedules so full
Instant gratification; the only rule
we followed in our quest for more
swiping left when we felt bored

Until a virus stopped us in our tracks
that's when we began to see the cracks
Forced to slow down and look at our life
face who we are; our struggles and our strife

This life lockdown comes with blessings
take time to reflect; there are valuable lessons
That if learned can enhance our life
gratitude in place of strife

Life Lesson – Slowing Down

When the world experienced the Pandemic in 2020, life changed for everyone. For the first time, there were government enforced rules and restrictions that affected our freedom. Preventing us from living our lives, or travelling, and leaving our homes was prohibited.

As a collective, we experienced so many emotions, fear, anger, frustration, and shock. We were forced to slow down, to take time out from our fast-paced life of instant gratification and quick fixes. Slowing down meant that there was time to stop and think about how we were living our lives.

We began to question if we were happy with our career, our life choices, and the way we were treating ourselves and others. The merry-go-round of life had been spinning so fast, we had forgotten we could actually get off if it were not making us happy anymore.

This Life Lockdown comes with blessings; by slowing down, we had time to think about our life. If our life was not going in the right direction, we had time to consider how we could change things. It also allowed us to stop and really appreciate what we have, our health and our families.

To see that life is precious and to not take it for granted. To move forward with a new sense of purpose and appreciation for the gift of life.

Self-Enquiry Questions – Slowing Down

Did you get the opportunity to 'slow down' during lockdown?

_____
_____
_____
_____

How did you feel about slowing down?

_____
_____
_____
_____

On reflection, did you learn anything about yourself?

_____
_____
_____
_____

Did you make any changes in your life as a result?

_____
_____
_____
_____

Start with the End in Mind

If you don't know where you are going
how will you know you've arrived?
Without a goal or purpose
is it possible to thrive?

Take time to visualise your future
what you want and how it would feel
Be clear and set your intentions
dream big - imagine it's real

You don't need to know how to get there
just start, each step will become clear
If you start with the end in mind
what you visualise will appear

Life Lesson – Having a Vision for Life

Having goals and a sense of purpose helps you achieve what you want in life. Consider successful people; they often have a vision of what they want to achieve, and they set out to make it happen for them.

Many people go through life without a clear vision of what they want to achieve. There may be a number of reasons for this; they may have limiting beliefs about what they can achieve, or they may have been conditioned to believe that their goals or dreams were unrealistic; that they should be happy with what they have.

We have a huge capacity to create the life we want to live; the first step is to take the time to visualise what you want and how it would feel if you had it. By setting a clear intention about what you want to achieve, you can start to consider all the steps required to achieve your dream.

Many people get overwhelmed at this stage. The jump between where they are and where they want to be can seem too big, but if you break it down into smaller, manageable steps it is more achievable and less scary. Sometimes the secret is just to take one step. Then the next step becomes clearer and before you know it, what you visualised will appear.

Self-Enquiry Questions – Having a Vision for Life

What goal would you like to achieve?

_____
_____
_____
_____

What is stopping you from achieving this goal?

_____
_____
_____
_____

How would it feel if you achieved this goal?

_____
_____
_____
_____

What small step could you take to work towards your goal?

_____
_____
_____
_____

Go Within

We spend our life looking outwards
for the things that we desire
We can travel around the world
for answers we may never acquire

Yet what if the answers we seek
are there inside our mind
If we push out all the distractions
and leave the past behind

The key to our success lies within
if we have faith and believe
We all have the ability to manifest
whatever we want to achieve

Life Lesson – Connecting to Intuition

We have a tendency in life to seek answers from outside of ourselves. We look to friends, family, teachers, mentors, and other people we believe will know better than us. Those with life experience, professional experience or people who we aspire to be like.

There is nothing wrong in seeking advice from others, but it is important to remember that we are also able to connect with our own intuition and inner knowing.

In order to connect with our intuition, we need to quiet the noise and distractions. Taking a walk outside in nature, listening to relaxing music or meditations are all ways for us to quiet our mind. When the mind is quiet, we are better able to connect with our intuition.

Another helpful way to connect with our intuition is to simply sit with a notepad and ask questions to our self, writing down whatever answers come to mind. In the process of enquiring, true inner wisdom can be revealed.

Inside you are all the answers you need – you simply need to have faith in yourself and believe. If you do, you can manifest whatever you want to achieve in your life.

Self-Enquiry Questions – Connecting to Intuition

Do you seek answers to life challenges through other people?

_____

_____

_____

_____

Have you connected to your intuition when seeking answers and has this been effective?

_____

_____

_____

_____

If you have not connected to your intuition, try the following steps, and see what is most effective for you.

Ask a question and then meditate on the answer

_____

_____

_____

Ask a question and then write down the answer in a journal

_____

_____

_____

Ask a question and then contemplate whilst walking in nature

_____

_____

_____

Reflections

When I look in the mirror, who do I see?
Whose reflection is staring back at me?
The daugher, sister, mother or wife?
We are so many versions of ourselves in life

Am I the woman who tries to get it all right?
Or the girl who used to party all night?
Am I the mother teaching her daughter self-esteem?
Or the little girl who loved to day dream?

Maybe I am all those versions
Each version taught me valuable lessons
So I'll embrace all sides of me
Anu welcome new chapters that are still to be

Life Lesson – Reflecting on Who We Are

When we take time to reflect on our life, we recognise that we have been many versions of ourselves; a child, an adult, a girlfriend/boyfriend, a wife/husband, a parent. We may have been the shy one, the loud one, the wild child, the dreamer, the extrovert, the life and soul of the party.

Reflecting on our life gives us the opportunity to recognise the lessons we have learned along the way. If you were an introvert, you may have become very good at listening and observing, and you will have a tendency to notice body language and subtle shifts in energy.

You will notice what others may not. If you were an extrovert, you may have had a tendency to lead and to show others how to live life to the full and embody who they are. If you were a wild child, you may have learned how to take risks and also the consequences of doing so. If you were a dreamer, this may have taught you to dream the things you want into existence and create your dreams.

We are never too old to create new versions of ourselves. Every version of who we are teaches us valuable life lessons. If we can embrace all aspects of who we have been, who we are now and who we want to become, then we can be open to embracing all that is yet to come.

Self-Enquiry Questions – Reflecting on Who We Are

How do you think your life has shaped who you are?

_____

_____

_____

_____

What has been the most valuable lesson you have learnt?

_____

_____

_____

_____

What new chapters of your life would you like to welcome?

_____

_____

_____

_____

Ancestral Wisdom

Deep within your mind
there is wisdom you can find
If you quiet the distractions
and are willing to take action

Connect to your inner knowing
if you trust you will be shown
What our ancestors learned before
that knowledge is at our core

So step into your power
use your knowledge to empower
Move forward with your wisdom
and trust your intuition

Life Lesson – What can we learn from our past?

We all embody the characteristics of our ancestors. It is in our DNA and embodied in the family traditions passed down through the generations.

We may have an entrepreneurial streak that runs back many generations; creativeness and vision, a belief that hard work pays off and the determination to make our vision a reality.

Or a tendency towards healing and helping others; we may be in a caring or spiritual profession, and it is likely that our ancestors were too, and this has influenced each generation.

If our ancestors experienced trauma and the habits associated with trauma, such as addiction, this can also be passed down the ancestral line. This does not mean that we are pre-destined to continue these patterns. Each generation is capable of breaking the chains so that future generations do not face the same challenges.

We have the opportunity to learn from previous generations; by slowing down and taking the time to connect with our intuition. We can also connect to the wisdom of those who went before us. To enhance our lives or to learn the lessons and break the chains to ensure a better outcome for future generations.

The choices we make on how we choose to live our lives will have a direct impact on future generations. It is important that we bear that in mind and make choices that will enhance those future generations.

Self-Enquiry Questions – What can we learn from our past?

What family characteristics have you inherited?

_____
_____
_____
_____

Are there family traditions that have been passed down within your family?

_____
_____
_____
_____

What (if anything) have you learned from previous generations?

_____
_____
_____
_____

If you share something with future generations, what would it be?

_____
_____
_____
_____

@Home

If our life is a reflection
of the home in which we live
Could our home gives us clues
to what we manifest and give?

Is our home a place of comfort
where we relax and feel at ease?
Or is it a cluttered and busy space
where we've adapted and appeased?

@Home

If our home isn't how we want it to be
it's time to de-clutter, freshen up and see
If we're willing to do the same with our mind
we'll make space for new experiences to find

As beauty doesn't always come at a price
we all have ability to create our dream life
First we must de-clutter and create the space
be open to the life that's there to embrace

Life Lesson – What does our Home say about us?

For many of us, our homes are very important. Home is a place where we spend a lot of our time, so it is no surprise that our homes tell us a lot about who we are as a person.
If comfort is important to us then our home will reflect that and when we step inside, we will feel comforted. If style is important to us, then our home may be a visual representation of our sense of style. If we like things minimal and simple, then our home will be that way.

If our homes are so closely linked to who we are as a person, can they give us some clues as to how we are feeling inside? If our home is feeling cluttered and a little run down, could this be a sign that we are feeling the same? Is it possible that we are not looking after ourselves as well as we should?
We get so busy with life that we do not always stop and take time to think about how we are actually feeling. If our home needed some attention to get it back to its best, we would take the time to do the work; we would buy the paint and give it a good clean and freshen up.

We need to remember to do the same for ourselves. If we have not been doing so, then we need to find time for some self-care. This can be as simple as recognising what requires attention and then giving that to yourself. It could be better sleep, some healthy eating or simply taking time to examine how you are feeling, perhaps through journaling or by spending time with someone you can talk to and share your feelings with. A self-care makeover is just as important as a home make-over.

Self-Enquiry Questions – What does our Home say about us?

What does your home say about you?

_____
_____
_____
_____

Can you see any connections between your home and how you feel at present?

_____
_____
_____
_____

What (if anything) could you do to improve your home?

_____
_____
_____
_____

If you made the changes, how would that feel?

_____
_____
_____
_____

Shadows

We all have shadows but are we aware
or are we racing through life too busy to care?
Ignoring the shadows we don't want to see
when facing our shadows can set us all free

Shadows are emotions we don't want to feel
yet pushing them away won't make them less real
By pushing them away, we are holding on tighter
by acknowledging them, we begin to feel lighter

As shadows are clouds with silver linings
behind the clouds the sun is always shining
Acknowledge your shadows and set them free
and make space for all that you can be

Life Lesson – Awareness of our Shadow Self

We all have our shadow sides; those parts of ourselves that we do not want to acknowledge or see. The emotions that want to push away when they arise, jealousy, competitiveness, anger, and fear. Emotions that do not feel good and that we do not want the world to see in us.

As children, we may have been told that displaying certain emotions was bad; so we started internalising those emotions as part of 'who we are' rather than just an emotion that we may feel from time to time. This results in us carrying around a deep sense of shame. We feel such resistance to certain emotions that we push them away and are unaware of our shadows.

Yet bringing our shadows into the light and acknowledging them can lead to real transformation. It feels difficult at first; especially if you have pushed away those feelings for a long time.

You need courage and an open heart. But by facing our shadow self, we can begin to break unhealthy cycles of behaviour, improve relationships with those around us and most importantly, improve our relationship with ourselves. If we take the time to do this work, it will impact positively on all the relationships in our lives.

Self-Enquiry Questions – Awareness of our Shadow Self

Do you have any shadow emotions you do not like to show?

_____
_____
_____
_____

When these emotions arise, where do you feel this in the body?

_____
_____
_____
_____

What can you learn from the emotions that arise from your shadow self?

_____
_____
_____
_____

Could acknowledging your shadow emotions enhance your life in any way?

_____
_____
_____
_____

Lessons

We teach our children lessons
to help guide them through life;
to share, be kind and helpful
and navigate through strife

Yet for everything we teach them
if we are open, we will learn
As children can see the beauty in life
we are too busy to discern

Children live for the moment;
they find joy in simple things
We have much to learn from our children
and all the blessings they bring

Life Lesson – Learning from Children

Many of us believe that as adults, our role is to teach our children, nieces, nephews, and grandchildren lessons that will guide them through life. Whilst this is true, and we do have a responsibility to support and guide them, we should also recognise that we can learn a lot from children.

Children teach us so much; they live for the moment and see joy in simple things. They feel their emotions fully; if they are upset or angry, they express that emotion in the moment but afterwards they are right back to feeling happy and having fun.

Children are authentically themselves; they display all their emotions openly; good and bad. They are not trying to be something that they are not. Often as adults we hold onto our emotions by pushing our feelings down and then wondering why we feel bad. Often, not feeling good is a sign of too many emotions that have never been expressed.

Children show us how to be authentic, how to be in the moment, how to feel our feelings and how to be free.

Spending time with them and observing how they interact is a great reminder of how to see things for what they are and not what we have projected them to be. By connecting to our inner child, we can see beauty and joy in life and that is truly a gift.

Self-Enquiry Questions – Learning from Children

What have you learned from children in your life?

_____

_____

_____

_____

How could you use what you have learned to enhance your life?

_____

_____

_____

_____

Write down childhood characteristics that brought you joy?

_____

_____

_____

_____

Could you integrate these characteristics to your life now?

_____

_____

_____

_____

Manifesting

We are all manifestors in life
we create our blessings and our strife
Most of us are not even aware
too busy with life to stop and care

But what if we took time to listen
to connect with our intuition?
Got clear on what we want to achieve
set clear intentions and believe

Trust in ourselves and know there is more
if we are willing to just open the door
We can make our dreams come true
by having faith and following through

Life Lesson – The Power of Manifesting

Every one of us has the ability to manifest. However, many of us are unaware of this capability. We assume life happens to us and that good fortune is a matter of luck; some people have it, others do not.

Yet we unconsciously manifest every day. When we walk into work thinking 'I wonder what drama or problem will present itself today' or when we think 'people always let me down,' we are in fact manifesting those thoughts into our reality.

Unconscious manifesting also works for the person that says, 'I can eat whatever I want and not gain weight' or 'I'm always really lucky.' They think it, believe it and as a result, manifest it.

When we understand the power of manifestation it is truly transformational. We realise that we have the ability to transform our dreams into reality. We just need to take the time to be clear about what we want, set our intentions, and have faith that we can receive.

We must also be aware of our language and habits, and recognise where we are manifesting what we do not want. Having awareness helps us shift our focus away from what we do not want, to what we do want and teaches us to trust that we all have the ability to manifest our thoughts into reality.

Self-Enquiry Questions – Manifesting

What have you manifested into your life?

_____

_____

_____

_____

What would you like to manifest into your life? (Be clear about what you want)

_____

_____

_____

_____

Tips to Manifest

- Be clear about what you want to manifest.
- Imagine how it would feel when you have manifested and hold that vision in your mind.
- Create a plan or vision board to draw in what you want to attract. Your vision board can include pictures of the things you want to attract.
- Trust the process and do not let fear distract you from manifesting. Acknowledge the fear and let it go.
- Be grateful for what you have already and be grateful for what you are manifesting (before and after you have received it).
- Make time to meditate to raise your vibration. The higher your vibration the easier it is to manifest.
- Acknowledge any signs from the Universe and follow your intuition.

Life Cheerleader

You are a special person in life
here to help and shine your light
To empower others and help them believe
that what they desire, they can achieve

By bringing light to the shadows
you share with others what you know
That when we face what we fear
our inner courage will appear

So keep being you and sharing your wisdom
and embrace all adventures still to come
Knowing that by simply sharing your light
you are helping people to ignite

Life Lesson – Inspirational People and Role Models

This poem was written for all the lovely people who are always there for other people, who motivate and inspire others and help them see that they have more potential than they believe.

The kind of people who help other people feel good by just being themselves – they are true Life Cheerleaders!

Life Cheerleaders offer support and encouragement and help others to see that many of the perceived blocks and barriers that hold us back in life are internal. We hold onto self-limiting beliefs from childhood; the feeling of not fitting in, being different to others, too quiet, too loud, too much. Although we grow up, we often still believe these thoughts internally and they can hold us back from being the best version of ourselves.

Life Cheerleaders are often able to see past those self-limiting beliefs and see in others all the things they do not see in themselves. They can help, inspire, and motivate us to move past our fears, encouraging us to take small steps. Before we know it, we are doing and achieving what we never thought possible.

To all the Life Cheerleaders; teachers, coaches, motivators, and lovely people with big hearts. Thank you for sharing your light and helping so many people ignite.

Self-Enquiry Questions – Inspirational People and Role Models

Who has been a life cheerleader in your life?

_____
_____
_____
_____

Have you been a life cheerleader in someone else's life?

_____
_____
_____
_____

What do you think are the characteristics of a life cheerleader?

_____
_____
_____
_____

Could you integrate these characteristics to your life now?

_____
_____
_____
_____

Lightworker

A spiritual healer, your colours so bright
codes taken inwards, transmitted to light
Vibrational energy taken in through a ray
to help others and guide the way

With the wisdom of ancestors as your guides
you shine light on the truth that others hide
That the answers we seek are there in our mind
if we quiet the noise, be patient and kind

Your guidance inspires and lights the way
for people who struggle to get through the day
So keep being you and shining your light
helping others find a spark of hope to ignite

Life Lesson – Respect for Spiritual Beings

Lightworkers come from all walks of life; different countries and diverse cultures; they show up in different ways. The one thing that Lightworkers have in common is an inner calling to help others.

Lightworkers may be teachers, health professionals, healers, wise men or woman, psychics, mediums, or spiritual teachers. We will all have come across someone in our life who has these attributes. It could be a friend, acquaintance, family member, parent, or a child.

Lightworkers are able to connect to their intuition and channel collective consciousness. They can provide guidance, support, and encouragement, helping others to connect with their own inner knowing and consciousness.

Lightworkers tend to be sensitive and may have experienced difficulties in their own lives, especially in their younger years.

They feel empathy for others as they have often felt pain themselves. Their purpose is to help others and help heal the collective. To make the world a little bit better, a little kinder and more compassionate.

Lightworkers elevate mankind's collective consciousness and if you are lucky enough to know or be a Lightworker then you are truly blessed.

Self-Enquiry Questions – Respect for Spiritual Beings

Who has helped you or those around you?

_____
_____
_____
_____

What qualities or characteristics did this person have?

_____
_____
_____
_____

Do you have any of these qualities or characteristics?

_____
_____
_____
_____

What have you done or what could you do to help others?

_____
_____
_____
_____

Kindness

Always keep in mind
it costs nothing to be kind
You can change someone's day
by thinking about the words you say

As the words we speak have power
cruel words do not empower
So if you have nothing to say
a smile can brighten someone's day

Kindness

As sometime people hide
what they feel inside
By showing someone that you care
a little kindness can be shared

So lets all be more self-aware
and maybe we could dare
to spread kindness to those we know
and maybe make more friends not foes

Life Lesson - Kindness

Kindness does not cost a thing yet offering a little kindness to someone can make all the difference in that person's day. We never know what is going on in someone's life and a little act of kindness may be all they need to get them through the day.

A kind teacher can make all the difference to the life of a child who is struggling. Those kind words may be the only gentle words that the child has ever heard, and that simple act of kindness offers hope. Hope that there are good people in the world and that things can get better.

Words hold a lot of power, so it is important to be aware of the language we use. If the things we say are not empowering, then we need to stop and consider why we are using that language and those words.

Kindness starts with us; if we are not kind to ourselves, how do we begin to show kindness to others? If we start to make some time for self-care and compassion towards ourselves then this will help us to see and feel the benefits of kindness. By feeling the benefit, ourselves, we are more likely to be able to have compassion and kindness for others.

In the world we live in, there is much fear, uncertainty, and pain. If we all took the time to be kind to ourselves and kind to others, we could begin to change the world.

Self-Enquiry Questions – Kindness

Who do you know that embodies kindness?

_____

_____

_____

_____

Has anyone shown kindness to you in your life?

_____

_____

_____

_____

How did that kindness make you feel?

_____

_____

_____

_____

Can you think of a time when you have shown kindness to others?

_____

_____

_____

_____

You are not alone

You are not alone
just pick up the phone
When emotions get too much to bear
remember there are people who care

People who care about you
and know what you have been through
You don't need to live in the past
embrace your life – It goes so fast

Keep being true to you
and you will find your way through
Talk to friends, vent or moan
but always remember, you are not alone

Life Lesson – Feeling Disconnected

We can be in a room full of people, surrounded by friends and family and still feel alone. We can appear to the world like we have it all together whilst inside we are falling apart.

Feeling alone feels empty, and when you have felt that feeling for too long, you cannot see how you will get through it, or if things will ever change. But you are not alone, there is always someone who can help, someone that can offer support and advice and help you to see things differently.

There is huge healing in opening up to someone; a friend, a family member, or a counsellor. You may believe that nobody would understand, or want to hear how you feel, but sharing your feelings and emotions will help you to release them. A problem may seem difficult to overcome in your head but sharing and discussing your feelings with someone can help you gain a sense of perspective.

Journaling can be very powerful in helping process your feelings. Getting your emotions out onto paper can help you view them from another angle. Joining online groups with other people who are feeling alone or experiencing the same kind of emotions as you. can help you realise you are not alone. You may discover that you know how to deal with certain emotions that others are struggling with too.

Connecting and helping others can also feel really transformative and help you to heal.

There is power in reaching out and talking. There are always people who will listen. You are not alone!

Self-Enquiry Questions – Feeling Disconnected

Have you ever felt disconnected?

_____
_____
_____
_____

Where did you feel this in your body?

_____
_____
_____
_____

Where do you think this feeling came from?

_____
_____
_____
_____

What did you learn from this?

_____
_____
_____
_____

Love

Love is the spark that ignites the fire
lifts your emotions, makes you feel inspired
Slowly melts the layers around your heart
opens you up: cold heart departs

But love must always be treated with care
you cannot lock it up or be scared to share
Doing this will not make love thrive
trust and freedom, keeps love alive

So if you are lucky to be blessed with love
you already have enough
Treat it well and always be kind
as love is not always easy to find

Life Lesson – Love

Love makes the world go round and there is no doubt that love has powerful and transformational properties. Love is the reason for many beautiful things in life; friendship, a love affair, a marriage, a child or children, a family. Love is a beautiful thing and should be treasured.

Sometimes, when people experience love, the feelings are so strong and intense that they experience fear at the thought of losing the love they have found. When this happens, there is a tendency to lock down that love, in an effort to try and keep it.

This can be detrimental because love is not a possession; it cannot be owned. It should be nurtured, cared for, and appreciated.

Some people crave the feeling of love, but fear being hurt.

They may have loved before and been hurt, or they may never have been shown love as a child and do not believe themselves to be worthy of love. As a result, they see love as something scary, or something that is always out of reach.

Some people may have experienced a great love in their life but lost it. They may be grieving for their lost love, which might be for more than one person; it could be a parent, a partner, or a child. However, you never truly lose love – that person may no longer be there in the physical sense but the love you shared is stored within your heart and can never be lost.

Whatever form of love you have or have had in your life – be grateful for that experience. Cherish it and hold it in your heart.

Self-Enquiry Questions – Love

Have you experienced love in your life?

_____
_____
_____
_____

How did that feeling of love make you feel?

_____
_____
_____
_____

Do you feel a sense of self-love towards yourself?

_____
_____
_____
_____

If not, what could you do to be more loving to yourself?

_____
_____
_____
_____

Fear

It can start slowly
or come out of the blue
At times you are not aware
that fears crept up on you

A racing heart, a feeling of dread
a wish to hide away in bed
Trying to be safe wont keep fear away
the more you hide; the longer it stays

Yet what is fear
but a thought in our mind
that's taken root and grown wild
leaving us upset and riled

Fear

How do you make fear depart?
Go inside and connect to your heart
By slowing down and taking time to listen
you can connect to your intuition

As we all have courage in our heart
to face the fears that are holding us back
Facing our fear takes away its power
by doing so we begin to empower

Ourselves and know that we are strong
and fears that held us back were wrong
Facing our fear shows us the way
for many more brighter days

Life Lesson – Facing Fear

Most of us experience fear at some point in our lives. For some people fear is something that has been present all of their life and they may feel it has held them back. For others, fear is the driver behind their success; they do not consider failure to be an option. They choose to use fear as a driver, to help them overcome all obstacles.

It is easy to let fear hold you back. When the emotion of fear appears in the body it is very common to want to run from the feeling and avoid whatever triggered that fear. This is counterintuitive though, as sometimes we need to stop and face the fear without retreating. If we slow down and connect with our intuition, we can begin to understand what is triggering the fear.

Acknowledging and naming the emotion is a great first step. For instance, by saying "I see you fear – I know you are trying to keep me safe, but I will be okay", we are acknowledging that the fear is not who we are. We are just feeling an emotion in the moment, and by recognising and naming the emotion, we are taking away its power to hold us back or keep us stuck. If what you are fearing cannot harm you, then take small steps towards doing what you fear. That alone will point you in the right direction.

There is a saying that it is useful to keep in mind; 'feel the fear and do it anyway'. It is a reminder not to run away from your emotions, but to acknowledge them and then proceed anyway. By doing so, we often realise that what we were fearing was not actually as bad as we thought, we had just built it up to be insurmountable in our mind. The more we face our fears the braver we will become and the more confident we will feel.

Self-Enquiry Questions – Facing Fear

Have you experienced fear in your life?

_____
_____
_____
_____

Where do you feel fear in your body?

_____
_____
_____
_____

Where do you think you fear comes from?

_____
_____
_____
_____

What have you learned about yourself through experiencing fear?

_____
_____
_____
_____

Grief

How do you recover from grief
when it steals your joy like a thief?
When you awake with pain inside your heart
how can you make that feeling depart?

Avoiding the pain will not drive it away
the more you avoid the longer it will stay
Honouring your feelings is all you can do
allow the grief to wash over you

Your grief is a measure of your love
make space for it, wear it like a glove
Honour your feelings and the pain will lessen
the love that you shared will be your blessing

Life Lesson – Making Space for Grief

Grief is something that we all experience at some point in our lives. When you feel grief, you know you have experienced love; the loss of that love creates the feeling of grief and that feeling can be overwhelming.

Grief is often associated with death; however, you can experience grief without the physical death of someone. You can also experience grief at the end of a relationship or friendship that was very important to you.

There are many emotions that arise when experiencing grief; denial, anger, depression, or a feeling of numbness. Everyone experiences grief in their own way. It is not a linear process, there are ups and downs along the way.

It is natural, especially in the early days, to want to avoid your feelings. They feel so intense and painful. Whilst you may be able to avoid your feelings for a while, the intensity of the emotions will not lessen until you allow yourself to actually feel them.

By feeling every emotion, you are not only honouring your grief, but also love that you shared. Your grief is a measure of your love. With time, the intensity of your grief will ease, and you will be able to move forward with your life, whilst always honouring the person you loved.

Self-Enquiry Questions – Making Space for Grief

Have you experienced grief in your life? *This could be grief over losing a loved one, a job, a friendship.*

_____

_____

_____

_____

Where did you feel the emotion within your body?

_____

_____

_____

_____

Did you learn anything about yourself through the experience of grief?

_____

_____

_____

_____

What could you do to honour your grief?

_____

_____

_____

_____

Searching

Waking up through the night
with nothing on my mind
Yet I feel like I am searching
for something I can't find

Searching my mind for answers
to a question I don't know
The hours spread out in front of me
and time passes so slow

Before I know it morning comes
and the promise of a new day
So I focus on my blessings
and move forward in my own way

Life Lesson - Searching

We spend so much of our life searching; for the perfect partner, the dream job, for purpose, excitement, escape, our dream home. There is no end to what we search for.

With today's technology we can search for anything; it is all at the tip of our fingers and the list of what we are searching for grows daily. We are bombarded by adverts telling us what we need; the latest gadget, the skincare that will transform you, the dream holiday.

Some people travel all around the world searching. But what if we took time off from searching to stop and ask why? Why are we always searching and why, when we find what we are searching for, does the feeling of satisfaction only last for a moment and then we are onto the next thing?

We spend our time looking outside of ourselves for the answers. Is it possible that what we are searching for is already within us? If we slow down a little, take time to contemplate and reflect then maybe the answers to the questions we have will be revealed through our own intuition.

Is it possible that we are really just searching for connection and if we connect with who we are at a soul level we might just find what we were searching for all along? Connection to self.

Self-Enquiry Questions – Searching

What are you searching for in life?

_____

_____

_____

_____

How do you think it would feel if you found what you were
searching for?

_____

_____

_____

_____

What emotion or need would be met by getting what you are
searching for?

_____

_____

_____

_____

Could you give yourself what you are looking for?

_____

_____

_____

_____

Beach Walks

Walks down the beach in the pouring rain
allows me a moment to connect to my pain
To sit with it and not run away
to honour my emotions and know it's okay

To reflect on memories of times gone by
and allow myself the space to cry
As the rain pours down and I look above
walks down the beach help me feel the love

Life Lesson – Connecting with Nature

There is nothing more grounding than connecting with the elements. There is something about the beach and the ocean that helps connect us to our inner emotions.

The roar of the sea on a stormy day can feel reassuringly comforting when we are experiencing stormy emotions inside.

The sea does not contain itself; it can be wild, stormy, and relentless one day and peaceful, serene, and calm the next.

No apology given.

The sea air is refreshing; it blows away the cobwebs and clears our mind in the same way. The noise of the waves hitting the shore can be as calming to the mind as meditation.

The beach is like an old friend; always there, consistent, and reliable. There is no need to talk or explain, you can just be there, with your thoughts and feelings. You can show up uninvited when you need to, and it is always okay.

The sea air can blow away your tears on a stormy day or can settle you with its stillness. The smell of the beach is very earthy and will help you to feel grounded and connected to nature.

The beach is one of nature's gifts and even if you can only visit for a day, it is a gift that always gives.

Self-Enquiry Questions – Connecting to Nature

Where do you go to connect with nature?

_____
_____
_____
_____

How do you feel when you connect to nature?

_____
_____
_____
_____

Do you use this time to contemplate or think?

_____
_____
_____
_____

How could you build time to be in nature more?

_____
_____
_____
_____

Living with Grief

Learning to live with grief in your life
is like feeling your way round the edge of a knife
Some days there is sunshine and life carries on
and then you feel sad and your joy has gone

You wonder if you will ever feel the same
if there is an end to this feeling of pain?
Your mind plays memories from the past
like a movie where you are the only cast

But hope is there beneath the pain
your loved one would want you to live again
Create new memories, live life to the full
as your loved one watches over you

Life Lesson – Living with Grief

Learning to live with grief can be difficult to navigate for most people, particularly in the beginning. Grief is an overwhelming feeling and takes up a lot of emotional energy.

In order to move forward in your life, you need to try and make space for your grief, whilst still having the emotional capacity to deal with life and its everyday challenges. This can be hard to navigate at times; there will be good days and bad days and sometimes it will feel like there are more bad days than good.

It is common to believe that you will never feel the same again. The emotions feel so painful, and we tend to spend a lot of time in the past, reflecting on memories, wishing we could go back in time and re-live those moments. We may regret things we said or did, we may wish we had spent more time with our loved one or had taken the time to tell them how important they were to us.

But there is hope beneath the pain, it may not feel like there is, but we can start to move forward with our life. It does not mean we have forgotten about our loved one, they will always be in our heart. They would want us to create new memories and live life to the full, knowing that they are always around us on our journey through life, watching over us.

Self-Enquiry Questions – Living with Grief

How have you learned to live with grief in your life?

_____
_____
_____
_____

How have you allowed yourself to process your feelings of grief?

_____
_____
_____
_____

How could you move forward whilst honouring your grief?

_____
_____
_____
_____

What has living with grief taught you about yourself?

_____
_____
_____
_____

Hope

How do you begin to feel hope
when life has left you feeling broke?
When you wake each day feeling low
and you cannot seem to find your flow

Be grateful each day for the things that you love
for the air in your lungs and the sky above
Try to find joy in the simple things
and see what blessings life can bring

Be kind to yourself, take it day by day
embrace your emotions, do not run away
Before you know it, you will hope once more
and be open to new adventures to explore

Life Lessons - Hope

Hope – such a little word but it holds so much power and possibility.

Hope is what propels us forward; what motivates us to keep going in the face of challenges we experience in everyday life.

Hope gives us the encouragement to believe that better things are coming; the relationship we want, the child we yearn for, the dream job, our health and wellbeing. The list is endless.

Hope is so important; with hope there is a chance that things will change, get better, and improve.

When we lose hope, it feels grey; we feel resigned to the feeling that life is what it is and there is nothing we can do to change it. Some of the sparkle goes and we cannot see the blessings we have in life.

So how do you get hope back when you lose it? Start by being grateful for the little things. The more we focus on what we have, the more blessings we will notice, and hope will slowly return.

If we add a little faith to our hope, we have the power to transform that hope into reality. We may not always get what we want, but with hope, faith in ourselves and trust in the universe, we will receive what we need.

Self-Enquiry Questions – Hope

What brings you hope in life?

_____
_____
_____
_____

How has hope enhanced your life or helped you move
forward?

_____
_____
_____
_____

Have you been able to find hope after losing faith?

_____
_____
_____
_____

Write down one thing you hope for the future

_____
_____
_____
_____

A Poem for the Dads

From the moment your child is born
yours are the arms: loving and strong
Wiping the tears from their eyes
sharing with them all things wise

What they learn from you sets the tone
its your voice they hear when they"re alone
Encouraging words and time spent together
builds a relationship that can be treasured

To all the dads; here and gone
through your child your spirit lives on
Thank you for your love and care
loving memories to feel and share

Father and Father Figures

Fathers and father figures are very important in a child's life. If you have been lucky enough to have had a good father or father figure in your life then you will have gained so much from that relationship. You will have had a positive role model; someone who embodied important attributes such as wisdom, strength, courage, confidence, and self-esteem.

As a child you may have admired those qualities and wanted to emulate them yourself. Many boys who have a good father or father figure wanted to be like them when they grow up and many girls look for the same qualities and attributes in a boyfriend or husband.

The words you hear as a child are the words that you internalise, and those words become your inner voice. If you were encouraged to believe you could achieve, you will achieve. If you were shown kindness, you are likely to be kinder to yourself and to others.

No matter whether you had a good role model in your father or father figure, the important thing to remember are the lessons that you learned. If those lessons were positive then these can be repeated but if they were not then you can learn what not to do and to be a better role model yourself.

Self-Enquiry Questions – Fathers and Father Figures

How has your father or father figure influenced your life?

_____
_____
_____
_____

What has this taught you about yourself?

_____
_____
_____
_____

What lessons have you learned?

_____
_____
_____
_____

Does your inner voice reflect what you heard from your father/father figure?

_____
_____
_____
_____

The Day Things Fell Apart

We shattered into pieces
the day things fell apart
The words could not be taken in
and pain filled all our hearts

One minute you were there
the next thing you were gone
There was no time to process
we all felt so withdrawn

The Day Things Fell Apart

Shock made way for sadness
and we allowed grief to come in
We looked at pictures of happy times
and reflected on memories within

We'll keep you safe inside our hearts
until we meet once more
We know you'll be there to guide us
in a different way than before

Life Lesson – Moving through the Pain of Sudden Loss

Moving through and processing the pain of sudden loss can be very difficult. Initially you will feel shock; your mind unable to process the enormity of what has happened, and you may initially feel numb. You may appear calm on the outside but people may not know what to say or how to react around you.

During this stage, your mind allows you to process what has happened gradually, so as not to overwhelm you with the enormity of your feelings all at once. With each day that follows, it becomes a little more real. It is not unusual to want to talk about what happened over and over; this is a natural coping mechanism to allow yourself to further process your feelings.

When shock begins to wear off and you begin to feel acceptance of the situation, you will feel a deep sense of sadness. For the things you never got to say, for the silly arguments or disagreements. You may spend a lot of time thinking about your loved one, wondering if they knew how much you loved them and wishing you had spent more time with them.

Sudden loss teaches us that life is precious, and it can be gone in a second; it's a painful lesson but if we can learn from that pain, then maybe we can love those we have a little bit more, we can be a little braver, take a few more risks, live life to the full, and learn not be held back by things that do not really matter.

We can keep our loved one safe inside our hearts while trying to live our lives with some purpose; more compassion and kindness, knowing that they will be with us on our journey through life until it is time to meet again.

Self-Enquiry Questions – Sudden Loss

Have you experienced sudden loss? *This does not necessarily mean death but could also be abandonment or the sudden loss of something important.*

_____

_____

_____

_____

What impact did this have on you?

_____

_____

_____

_____

What did you learn about yourself through this experience?

_____

_____

_____

_____

Memories

Our life is a series of memories
of experiences we have had
Some memories make us happy
and others make us sad

Yet the beauty of our memories
is replaying the ones we treasure
Kept safe inside our mind
our memories last forever

So live life to the full
create memories along the way
As you'll always have your memories
they will never go away

Life Lesson – Make Memories

As humans we have a huge capacity to store memories in our minds. We can recall memories from every stage of our lives. some memories are happy and we like to relive them over and over again; weddings, birthdays, a first kiss.

We also hold onto memories that make us sad; memories of people no longer with us or situations we experienced in the past that made us sad or upset. We want to push away bad memories, but they sometimes appear in our minds uninvited.

The great thing about memories is that we have the ability to recall and play back the ones we treasure. We may choose to write them down in a journal or save them in a photo album so that we can call up our memories whenever we want.

Life is a series of memories so it is important that we remember to keep creating new experiences. One day those experiences will be our memories. Live life to the full, spend time with family and friends, try things you did not think you would, live a life that you will want to remember and look back on, feeling glad that you had those experiences.

Self-Enquiry Questions – Memories

Do you reflect on your memories?

_____
_____
_____
_____

Write down at least one memory that makes you feel happy?

_____
_____
_____
_____

What do you notice about yourself from the memory?

_____
_____
_____
_____

What could you learn from that memory that you can take forward in your life?

_____
_____
_____
_____

Behind the Masque

Behind the masque where nobody can see
there is another version of me
She's a little bit tired, a little less together
and a part of her has changed forever

Gone is the girl, young and carefree
who lived for the weekend and shopping sprees
Who secretly just wanted to fit in
whilst she partied in heels drinking gin

Yet the woman I am behind the masque
is a little more grounded, doesnt need to ask
for permission from others to be all that I am
so I take off the masque, knowing that I can

Life Lesson – Hiding behind a Masque

How many of us have worn a masque at some point in our life? We want to present ourselves as confident and outgoing when we do not feel that way on the inside. We 'power dress' believing that clothes will help us appear to be the confident businessman or woman we long to be.

We may have worn a masque to hide our vulnerability. Deep down we feel shy or sensitive but we put on a masque to convince the world that we are confident and outgoing. If we wear our masques well, we may fool people into believing we are something that we are not. We may even forget that we are wearing a masque.

Sometimes the weight of wearing a masque for too long gets too heavy to bear. Underneath the masque we feel tired and a little less together than we may have presented ourselves to be.

But what would happen if we decided to embrace who we are and take the masque off. What if what was beneath the masque, the true essence of who we are is actually more relatable and real than what we were pretending to be. We would be able to relax a little bit more, be more grounded and not require permission from others to be all that we are or wanted to be.

Self-Enquiry Questions – Hiding behind a Masque

Have you ever hidden behind a masque?

_____
_____
_____
_____

Why do you think you choose to do that?

_____
_____
_____
_____

How would it feel if you could take of the masque and show the world the real you?

_____
_____
_____
_____

Write down at least three qualities that you have that you like about yourself?

_____
_____
_____
_____

Journey to Self Love

Distractions, avoidance, schedules so full
pushing emotions away as a rule
Ignoring the inner voice in our mind
that's trying to tell us; slow down, be kind

But kindness is something reserved for others
our family, friends, partners or lovers
How did we forget to take care of ourselves
self-love like an old book, sat on the shelf

There comes a time when we're ready to change
when we look inside and it feels so strange
To hear how we speak to ourself is a shock
but having awareness can help us unblock

Journey to Self Love

As we let go of blockages and fears
emotions release and turn into tears
This creates a space for self-care
and as we grow, old patterns become rare

This is the journey to self-love
slow and steady like the wings of a dove
A range of emotions with each passing day
self-love is the compass to guide us on our way

Life Lesson – Self Love

If you are lucky enough to have grown up with a strong sense of who you are and have lived your life with a clear sense of purpose, then it is likely that you also have a healthy amount of self-love. There is a difference between self-love and 'loving yourself' which often has connotations of being arrogant or self-obsessed. Self-love is about taking care of yourself; your emotional and physical needs and having healthy boundaries.

For many people, self-love is something that has to be learned and there can be a journey to get there. We are often kinder to family and friends than we are to ourselves, meeting their needs and forgetting that we also have needs that require to be met.

We may choose to educate ourselves by reading self-development books or by attending self-development courses. What we learn through self-development allows us to review our patterns of behaviour and internal dialogue. It can be a shock when we realise that the thing that is holding us back in life is ourselves and our self-limiting beliefs.

By making a conscious decision to face who we are in the mirror; both the good and the bad aspects of our nature, we can break old patterns and begin to re-write the script. We can to start to address behaviours that are holding us back. The process can be hard work and may bring up emotions that we have been avoiding, but if we are brave and willing to do the work, we can achieve positive change, creating space for self-care, leading to self-love.

Self-Enquiry Questions – Self Love

Do you compare yourself to others and/or worry about other people's opinions?

_____
_____
_____
_____

Do you allow yourself to make mistakes and learn from them?

_____
_____
_____
_____

Do you believe your value is based on how you look or what you do for others?

_____
_____
_____
_____

Write down at least three strengths and qualities you possess?

_____
_____
_____
_____

What do you do to be kind to yourself?

_____
_____
_____
_____

What first step could you take towards self-love?

_____
_____
_____
_____

Soul Sisters

Free spirited soul sister
around the world you travel
Seeking different ways of life
new meanings to unravel

Coming home to ground again
taking time to discover
Spirital lessons along the way
that help you to recover

Soul Sisters

Making peace with the past
helps you close a chapter
Letting go of what no longer serves
makes room for love and laughter

Your spirit loves to be free
to seek out life adventures
To add to your book of life
memories to treasure

Life Lesson – Learning from Free Spirits

There are people in life who are free spirits; they see the world as a place to explore and choose not to be limited by the constraints that society puts upon them. They choose to explore who they are and are open to new experiences that will teach them more about themselves.

Most young children are free spirits; they are uninhibited and embrace life with complete freedom. But as they grow these characteristics can get lost; through conditioning at school or taught at home to be more responsible, told to avoid taking risks and to follow rules and guidance.

Free spirits tend to retain their childlike state and the joy that goes along with that. They may choose to travel around the world, exploring different countries and cultures with an open mind and sense of curiosity. They may choose to learn how other people live, they will try different cuisines and explore different ways of working and living.

Free spirits do not require approval from others – they trust their instincts and are guided by their intuition. They are sincere; true to who they are and are not trying to be something they are not.

If you are a free spirit – there is no doubt you will live life to the maximum and experience so much from life. But you will also influence those around you, especially those who are less free spirited than you. They will have the opportunity to learn from you and even live vicariously through you. Free spirits light the road ahead for others to see what is possible.

Self-Enquiry Questions – Free Spirits

Who is a free spirit in your life? *This could be you, a family member, or a friend*

_____
_____
_____
_____

What characteristics of a free spirit do you admire the most?

_____
_____
_____
_____

Do you see any of those qualities in yourself?

_____
_____
_____
_____

What can you learn from free spirits that you could integrate in your life?

_____
_____
_____
_____

Megan

A beautiful spirit, a beautiful soul
young and vibrant, but life took its toll
Good days and bad days, mixed into one
a mixture of sadness and days of pure fun

With so much to offer, and so much to give
an internal darkness pushed on your will to live
When the sun shone, it lifted your mind
yet through it all, you found time to be kind

Megan

Blessed with a mother, strong and true
who'd do what it took to help her girl through
The darkest days when you wanted to hide
she was always there, right by your side

Your mum keeps your memory alive
Megan's Space helps others seek help and thrive
Your inherent light now guides the way
a beacon to others who feel lost along the way

This poem was written for a beautiful young girl called Megan who lost her life at the age of 20. Her mother kept her memory alive by setting up a charity called Megan's Space to help young people struggling with their mental health

Life Lesson – Keeping Memories Alive to Help Others

When people experience great tragedy and loss in their lives, the pain that accompanies it feels overwhelming. It creates a void in your life which is difficult to fill. Some people try to fill the void by keeping busy or by avoiding it all together. Others deal with it by using their pain to help others.

The act of giving back can be very healing. When you have experienced loss, you learn ways to cope and process these feelings. You also learn what does not work and this knowledge, when shared with others, can offer support and help them find their way through difficult feelings and emotions.

You are better able to help and support others when you understand their feelings and can empathise with their pain. You can inspire others who are able to see how far you have come on your journey and give them hope for better days to come.

It is recognising that the emotions you feel when you experience loss is equal to the amount of love that you felt for the person you lost. We try to avoid or quickly get past the feelings associated with loss but if we recognise these feelings as love, it is easier to accept and process these emotions.

Loss can be transformative; the pain of loss creates a huge amount of energy. If you can learn to accept and work with that energy, you can transform it into healing for yourself and others. And you can do all of that whilst keeping your loved ones memory alive, knowing that they are the inspiration to help others and to make the world a little better for it.

Self-Enquiry Questions – Keeping Memories Alive

How do you keep a loved one's memories alive?

_____
_____
_____
_____

What did you learn from that person that you could use to enhance your own life?

_____
_____
_____
_____

Write down at least three memories that you have of your loved one?

_____
_____
_____
_____

What characteristics live on in you that remind you of your loved one?

_____
_____
_____
_____

Find Your Calm

When life feels hectic, with so much to do
how can you make time for you?
With so many tasks that need to be done
where is the time to relax and have fun?

To find your calm, start by slowing down
its time to get off the merry-go-round
Make time each day to take care of you
and you'll be surprised at what you can do

Prioritise the things that you need to do
let go of things that make you feel blue
Connect to your breath and slow it down
and you'll feel calmness all around

Life Lesson – Find Your Calm

Life nowadays is very busy. We are required to fulfil multiple roles in life. The boss in the office leading a team; the parent organising family life and school trips, the other half in a relationship and the person helping friends.

With so much going on it is no surprise that it is difficult to find time to sit and relax. But it is possible; the simple act of sitting down and thinking about what you give your time to is the first step. The next step is to prioritise what is important. If you have no time for yourself but are spending hours on social media, consider whether this time can be better used for self-care rather than comparing your life to others on social media.

A morning routine can make a big difference to our day.

Getting up early before your children or family will allow some precious 'me time.' Use the time to meditate or set intentions for the day. This will energise you and give you a better start to the day as you will have taken care of yourself first.

Journaling is a really helpful way to process your day, giving you an opportunity to write down what went well, and note any challenges you encountered. This can be really therapeutic. Simply stop, reflect, and learn the lessons to enhance your life.

There can be a tendency to believe we do not have time yet most of the practices mentioned only require a small amount of time but can make a big difference to our life. If you can set 30 minutes aside most days for self-care, you will begin to feel better, and this will impact on all areas of your life.

Self-Enquiry Questions – Find Your Calm

What do you do to connect to your inner calm?

_____
_____
_____
_____

What sights and sounds make you feel most calm?

_____
_____
_____
_____

What makes you feel grounded and secure?

_____
_____
_____
_____

What could you do on a daily basis to make you feel calm?

_____
_____
_____
_____

About The Author

I am Sarah Barbour, a poet, writer and intuitive coach. I live in a small coastal town in Scotland with my husband and daughter.

I have worked for the NHS in Scotland for 25 years working in corporate roles; specialising in continual personal and professional development, education, quality improvement and project management. During this time, the development of people has been the most enjoyable and rewarding part of my career.

I started writing poetry during the COVID pandemic in 2021. I learned that poetry can help to process and unlock emotions. I enjoy working with people to help them connect to their emotions through my poetry and through 1:1 coaching.

I believe that we all have so much potential; we just need to learn to quite the external noise and connect to our inner wisdom.

Learn more about me:

Website: www.sarahbarbourcoaching.com

Instagram: @the_intuitive_poet

Facebook community:
www.facebook.com/groups/28093987444770

Printed in Great Britain
by Amazon

85762417R00081